Tiny
Goes to the
Library

by Cari Meister

illustrated by Rich Davis

HOUGHTON MIFFLIN   BOSTON

This is Tiny.

He is my best friend.

He goes where I go.

If I go to the park,
Tiny comes, too.

5

If I go to the lake, Tiny comes, too.

Today we are going to the library.

I get my library card.

I get my wagon.

Time to go!

Sorry, Tiny.

No dogs in the library.

You wait here.

I go inside.

Tiny stays outside.

I get dog books.

I get frog books.

I get bird books for Tiny.

I fill the wagon.

Tiny helps.

Oh no! Too many books!

I cannot pull the wagon.

Tiny can!